PEOPLE ENERGY PRINCIPLES

PEOPLE ENERGY PRINCIPLES

36 Reframes To Shift How You Think About People And Business

Alicia Parr

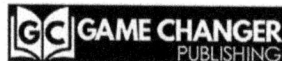

Published by Game Changer Publishing

Paperback: 978-1-967424-16-0
Hardcover: 978-1-967424-17-7
Digital: 978-1-967424-18-4

GAME CHANGER PUBLISHING
www.GameChangerPublishing.com

READ THIS FIRST.

Your journey to unleashing people energy starts here!

Scan the QR code below to access a special gift—What's available changes from time to time.
It might be an exclusive print (for the first 20 responders), early access to new insights,
or a Free People Energy audit to help amp your growth-readiness.

Don't miss out—Scan now and see what's waiting for you!

SCAN ME

PEOPLE ENERGY PRINCIPLES

36 REFRAMES

TO SHIFT HOW YOU

THINK ABOUT PEOPLE & BUSINESS

ALICIA J. PARR

PEOPLE ENERGY PRINCIPLES
36 REFRAMES TO SHIFT HOW YOU THINK ABOUT PEOPLE & BUSINESS

>   Foreword.   1

>   How to Read This Book.   3

1   A Business Is The Conversion Of
People Energy Into Economic Value.   5

2   First And Always, Stay In The Game.   6

3   Generally Speaking,
People Want To Do Good Work.   9

4   Unleash And Harness People Energy
— For Love And Truth.   10

5   Human Nature Isn't What We
Wish It Were — Act Accordingly.   13

6   Notice What People Say And
Believe What People Do.   17

7   Change People By Assuming
People Can't Change.   18

8   Every Human Is Uniquely Wired For Something.
It's Useful To Figure Out What That Is.   21

9   People Do Things For Reasons,
But Not Always The Reasons
They Give You.   22

10   Be Curious.
Share The Growth Mindset.   25

11   Every Solution Is First A Hypothesis.
Reality Test.   26

12   Real Skin In The Game
Creates True Accountability.   29

13   Personality Conflicts Aren't About
Personality. They're Organizational
Clarity Problems.   31

14   Apply The Trust Algorithm:
Accountability = Authority = Capability   32

15   Work Hard To Make Hard Things
(More) Simple.   35

16   Trust Comes After Cooperation.
In That Order.   37

17   Decisions Go Where They Belong.   39

18   Communication Is More Than
Saying Words.   40

19   Start Where The Other Person Is.   43

20   Co–author:
More Minds, More Better.   44

21   Don't Get Stuck
Addressing Symptoms.   47

22   Smallest Changes
For The Biggest Impacts.   48

23   Diagnose Before You Prescribe.   51

24   Prompt Grassroots
Decision–Making Often.   52

25   Sometimes There's One Right Way.
Probably Not This Time.   55

26   Feel Stuck?
Extend Your Time Horizon,
The View Is Different.   56

27   What We Know For Sure Is Tiny.
Blind Spots Are Many.   59

28   Manager Means Accountability
For Team Results.   61

29   Leadership Is Defined
By The Presence Of Followers.   63

30   When In Doubt,
Spread Accountability Out.   64

31   Same People In
Same Roles = Same Problems.   67

32   What We Do Is What We Believe.
Act On Purpose.   69

33   Build Systemic Liberty.   71

34   Watch Out For
The Decider Problem.   73

35   Gratitude Is Contagious.
Pass It On.   75

36   What's Old Is New Again. Again.   77

<   Appendix. The Trust Algorithm.   79

> FOREWORD.

Some people walk into your life as a matter of circumstance, but others? They arrive as if the universe itself has conspired to bring them to your doorstep at precisely the right moment. That's how I met Alicia Parr.

We were introduced by a mutual colleague at an executive luncheon, one of those polished affairs where handshakes are firm, conversations are measured, and introductions carry an air of expectation. Our colleague, eager to bridge the connection, launched into an attempt at describing Alicia's work—only to flounder mid-sentence. He started, hesitated, tried again, and ultimately surrendered with a half-smile, saying, *"You two ladies will figure it out."* And we did.

In mere seconds, Alicia and I found ourselves in an effortless exchange, one that felt more like a continuation of a conversation we had already been having for years rather than an introduction. She, a behavioral science nerd. Me, a human dynamics nerd. Both of us steeped in the world of human resources—hers rooted in people management and strategy, mine grounded in HR operations and organizational structure. It was as if two puzzle pieces had clicked into place, and from that moment forward, a professional respect and personal kinship were forged.

Alicia and I share an uncommon trait—we are both INTJs, a personality type that makes up just 2.1% of the global population. The rarity of that alone is something we marvel at, but the real magic lies in how our minds move in synchronized rhythm. We thrive on big ideas. We challenge assumptions. We are, by nature, architects of possibility. And yet, for all our shared intellectual curiosity, what bonded us most was the unshakable sense that our paths were meant to cross, that our connection was not just incidental but intentional.

Over the years, I watched Alicia's ideas evolve from casual conversations into something much larger. Her concept of "people energy" was not just an observation—it was a movement in the making. I loosely followed her adventures, taking note when she officially launched her company, Performentor. Every time our networks intersected, she would say with unwavering certainty, *"We're going to work together someday."* And I believed her. Not because the words were spoken, but because they carried the weight of inevitability.

Then, one day, Alicia shared a single sentence with me, *"A business is the conversion of people energy into economic value."* It stopped me in my tracks. There it was. The truth no one teaches in business school. The truth that governs every successful company. Business is not just about processes, systems, or profit margins—it is about people. Their energy, their innovation, their willingness to show up and give of themselves. Alicia had articulated something so fundamental yet so overlooked that it felt like a revelation. It was in that moment that I knew she wasn't just defining a concept. She was shifting a paradigm.

Alicia Parr is not a conventional thinker. She is a bold leader, a disruptor of the status quo, and an intuitive visionary. She is the kind of person who doesn't just see the future—she builds the blueprint for it. Throughout our friendship, I have had the privilege of being her muse, her sounding board, her confidant, and her peer. But most of all, I have been an agent of trust in her journey, someone who knew—before the world did—that she was onto something that would change the way we think about leadership and work.

This book, *People Energy Principles*, is more than a collection of insights. It is a call to action. It is the playbook for modern leadership. It is the guidebook for those who understand that the workforce is not a machine to be optimized, but an ecosystem to be nurtured.

If you are a leader, a business owner, or someone who believes that the future of work must be different from the past, this book belongs in your hands. Alicia's premise—*a business is the conversion of people energy into economic value*—isn't theory. It is the foundation upon which the next generation of business success will be built.

Olalah Njenga
CEO and Chief Strategist
YellowWood Group, LLC

Vice Chair and Small Business Designee
NCWorks Commission
State of North Carolina

> # HOW TO READ THIS BOOK.

Do you ever get stuck when trying to solve a problem? We all do. Yet, you already have access to more answers to more problems than you can imagine. They hide behind habitual thought patterns, unconscious beliefs about what's true, and the noise we subject ourselves to in the name of doing our job. It's finding your way to these answers that's the hard part.

This book aims to reconnect you with these hidden answers by offering thought prompts and reframing how people in organizations work and perform. It isn't a detailed "how-to" manual—plenty of those already exist. This book assumes that the right path forward in one situation isn't necessarily the right path forward in another—although you can gather clues about what to do from observing others and reading about "best practices."

This book provides **36 People Energy Principles** that help us think differently about people and business. The descriptions are brief so your mind can take an idea and build on it, applying it to whatever you are noodling on at the moment. You don't even have to read the whole section. If you read a few sentences and your mind wanders to how that might apply to something you are thinking about, that's a good thing.

In addition to the explanatory examples this book provides, the accompanying custom, hand-drawn artwork sparks inspiration and contemplation. Words provide stories, and visuals capture other parts of your brain. These prompts help you think outside the bounds of your current assumptions so you can navigate to better places.

The principles are presented in an order that attempts to build from foundational assumptions to more complex reframes, although following the order isn't necessary or even the right way to go for many situations and many people. This is because these principles are interdependent—meaning that they interact with each other and work together. There is no "right order."

This also means there's no wrong order in which to read this book—or wrong way! Start with the first principle or flip to the part that draws you in immediately. Follow your intuition and curiosity.

We all have boundaries that serve us well most of the time. Other times, our thought patterns and assumptions lead us into a mental cul-de-sac, where we get stuck. This book will help you find your way out of the cul-de-sac and back onto the highway with a new, higher-speed perspective.

ENJOY!

PEOPLE ENERGY PRINCIPLES
36 REFRAMES TO SHIFT HOW YOU THINK ABOUT PEOPLE & BUSINESS
A BUSINESS IS THE CONVERSION OF PEOPLE ENERGY INTO ECONOMIC VALUE.

1 A BUSINESS IS THE CONVERSION OF PEOPLE ENERGY INTO ECONOMIC VALUE.

"We have to decide between the people and the business." I've heard this sentence a lot. You probably have, too. Maybe you've said this or something like this. But what does it even mean?

This phrase usually implies a decision between sustaining near-term costs or passing the expense on to the employee base. It might be an explicit cost transfer in the matter of, for example, company contributions to health insurance. More often, we tell ourselves that the whole situation is one of spending money versus not spending it, as if those decisions have zero unintended consequences on the culture of trust and performance of the team.

But there *are* consequences.

People will allocate their commitment and effort in direct proportion to the commitment they feel from their employer. It's just a delayed effect—an indirect effect. So, it's easy to fool ourselves into thinking that money and people are two distinct parts of our organization.

What if we think about a business differently?

Another way to think about what a business is and does can help us view our teams, our success, and ourselves from a different perspective.

What if we consider a business as a dynamic process instead of a static idea? The dynamic process of converting human energy into sustained economic value.

Can you envision that? Consider what that implies about building a successful and healthy business! You want to unleash the people energy from each and every team member as much as possible. Additionally, you want to harness and guide that energy toward a meaningful, shared purpose. When you do those two things in a way that generates sustainable economic value, then you have a successful business.

What difficulties do you have today in your business? What changes if you re-think that challenge through this model of what a business is and does? What really is the source of your problem? Don't be surprised if the business world looks a little different when viewed this way.

2 FIRST AND ALWAYS, STAY IN THE GAME.

First and foremost, don't quit. Don't let the situation take you down. This principle stems from the idea of trying repeatedly, even with low odds of success, so long as you keep trying.

Let's say you have a 1-in-100 chance of winning. If you try it 100 times, the chances are you'll win at least once. Of course, some games can knock you out in a single round, like playing roulette by putting all of your chips on a particular number. Maybe, just maybe, you'll win big. If you get enough turns of the roulette wheel, you will eventually win so long as you don't run out of chips to bet with. Don't bet all your chips.

The key to being in it for the long haul is staying in the game for the long haul. You do this by making strategic decisions that maximize your upside and minimize your downside. Really minimize the downside. In other words, don't risk everything on a single uncertain payoff, no matter how tempting.

This principle applies in the business world as well. While you may have grand ideas and envision a world where everyone adopts your cutting-edge approach, the first step is to build something that works and convince a few people. Avoid moves that put you at risk of going out of business.

It takes time to change people's minds on a large scale. So, focus on developing a solid foundation, winning over a few early adopters, and gradually expanding your influence. Remember, staying in the game and steadily progressing is crucial for long-term success.

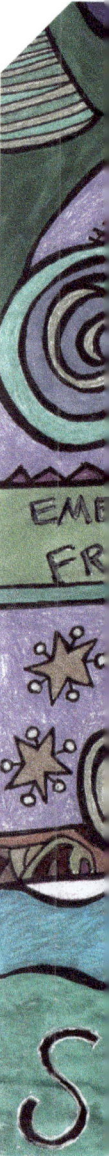

SEE ♦ APPEAR

BE COME

CONTEXT

current situation

NEAR FUTURE

DO ACT

THE EVERPRESENT FOUNDATION

OTHER

The Imagined

WAY FORWARD

PEOPLE ENERGY PRINCIPLES
36 REFRAMES TO SHIFT HOW YOU THINK ABOUT PEOPLE & BUSINESS
GENERALLY SPEAKING, PEOPLE WANT TO DO GOOD WORK.

3 GENERALLY SPEAKING, PEOPLE WANT TO DO GOOD WORK.

Do you think people have to be "motivated" to work? Will people sit around and do nothing, even if there's something meaningful for them to put their time and energy toward? Would you really spend the rest of your life doing nothing if you had the money?

I'm not talking about people who are in the pit of despair or under the influence of something that steals away their agency. These situations happen, sadly, too often. I'm not talking about the exceptions. I'm talking about *people in general*.

If your default assumption is that people must be watched every moment and prodded with carrots and sticks, or else they will do minimal work, where does that belief come from? What evidence do you have to support that belief? Does that assumption apply to you?

Perhaps you've heard about the research that compared student performance in two conditions: Teachers who were told that their students were gifted and bright, and teachers who were told that their students were below-average performers. The actual learning and performance outcomes strongly correlated with teacher expectations. The teachers who were told they had a gifted class *interacted with the students to generate that outcome*. And the reverse was true, too.

How does this pattern of belief come to life for business leaders? Your default belief about peoples' intrinsic motivations will shape how you interact with the team. If you assume that people generally want to do good work, what might change in how you think about why some succeed and some struggle in your business?

It becomes unnecessary to villainize anyone—to consider them poorly motivated or lazy. You begin to ask yourself questions such as the following:

Is the work designed properly?

Are the requirements described clearly?

Do people understand what's necessary?

Does the work contribute to the company mission?

Is there a rigorous removal of contrary incentives that make it harder to succeed?

Are different people/teams pitted against each other?

Are there systems of accountability in place?

You could ask more great questions, but this list should give you a good idea. So, let's try out a new assumption—that people, by and large, want to do good work. Then, put it into practice in your organization and see what changes. I think you'll be pleased.

4 UNLEASH AND HARNESS PEOPLE ENERGY — FOR LOVE AND TRUTH.

How do you feel when you are doing something well that you are good at? Amazing! How does it feel to be in a room of people when things are going well? It feels great! Now, how does the energy feel when things are blocked and not going well? Not good.

People energy. What is it?

People energy includes all the actions, decisions, ideas, and passion humans have and bring to bear. It swirls around us, through us, and between us. We've all heard the term "energy in the room." Is it high energy? Low energy? Positive energy? Angry energy? This isn't hocus pocus. You already *know* what people energy is.

Now that you get what people energy is, imagine the application of principle #1, a business as the conversion of this people energy into sustainable economic value.

The more you unleash the energies of each person's talents, interests, and skills, the more energy you have to harness for a particular purpose. The more you clarify how to work together towards a shared purpose, the more that purpose creates value for people. The more you focus the people energy within your organization, the healthier your business becomes.

Unleashing and harnessing people energy is potent. It really works.

When we think of these powerful influences, we want to be sure we're doing them for good and beneficial reasons. Too often, people use these techniques to gain power over others. To do that, they use a narrative that sacrifices truth and shifts power from one group to another.

If we prioritize power, we relinquish truth and love. We overrun the feeling of love with an intention to control others for our own privilege. Sometimes, that privilege is social. We want to show ourselves as "good people" by forcing others to behave in ways we prefer.

What if we aim for love and truth instead?

Real love—agape love—that we don't just reserve for people we agree with. Love is for all humans. True agape love is broad, expansive, and inclusive. We don't reserve it just for the people we agree with on all things. Seek this kind of love when unleashing and harnessing people energy.

The truth—not "my truth" or "your truth"—but THE TRUTH. Get the difference? One requires lots of humility. The other is selfish because framing a personal perspective as a form of "truth" is incorrect. Which one are you using?

Unleash people energy. Harness the energy. Play to win the really long game, and do it for love and truth.

PEOPLE ENERGY PRINCIPLES
36 REFRAMES TO SHIFT HOW YOU THINK ABOUT PEOPLE & BUSINESS
HUMAN NATURE ISN'T WHAT WE WISH IT WERE — ACT ACCORDINGLY.

5 HUMAN NATURE ISN'T WHAT WE WISH IT WERE — ACT ACCORDINGLY.

If only everyone were honest and ethical, *if only* all people were more empathetic, *if only* every human held the same values in the same proportions and order of priority as we do.

Imagine all the people living in harmony. It's easy if you try. Things would be so great.

But we humans don't roll that way. We are variable in our pre-wiring, tribal in nature, and products of our histories, genealogies, and embedded cultures.

We are individuals deciding for ourselves and are inextricably linked to the social structures we navigate. Both things are true simultaneously—for me, you, and every member of your team.

Do you know what a blank slate approach is? It's a belief that we are only and ever a result of our environment.[1] That we are born a blank slate, and the ONLY difference between different people's capabilities is their environment and the effort they've put into whatever it is they are learning and doing. Philosophers and thinkers have been puzzling over this for a long time. It's not a new idea. They called the idea tabula rasa earlier, but today, let's just call it a blank slate.

We are NOT born as blank slates.

We are all pre-wired to be more this or that or the other. We have default settings that are different from those of the next person. There is a tremendous opportunity to use that pre-wiring in all sorts of good or bad ways. But we are indeed pre-wired. The more we can take advantage of our own pre-wiring, the better.

Assuming we're all the same is wrong and inhumane.

One true thing about human nature is that our drive comes from a desire for affiliation and a certain level of acceptance by others. Some of us mind more than others, but everyone you'd ever want to work with will care about being accepted by others. You wouldn't want to work with them if they weren't concerned about social acceptance. Nobody would want to work with you if you didn't care about what other people think.

For that matter, when the urge to form connections is systemized into tribalism, there are good and bad aspects. Inter-tribe relations become tighter, and extra-tribe relations are treated negatively. The net result can be greater inter-group divisiveness. This happens no matter how empathetic, warm, and team-oriented a person is.

[1] Pinker, Steven. *The Blank Slate*. Penguin, 2003.

In fact, the more empathetic, warm, and team-oriented someone is, the more they'll justify themselves in defense of their tribe. This counterintuitive truth comes from a deep desire to care for one's own. Empathy can be selective!

When unhelpful tribalism happens within an organization, you can imagine how problematic that is. And wishing things weren't that way doesn't change it. Telling yourself that BAD people are the only ones who disagree with your preferred approach is false. It surely doesn't solve the problem.

You often see this in divisions between departments incentivized to pursue outcomes that conflict with each other. A sales team is incentivized to sell as high a volume as possible. A quality team is incentivized to eliminate quality problems. An engineering team is incentivized to create things that work. A production team must efficiently deliver things. While all of these departments must work together for the business to work well, it's normal and natural for these smaller teams to identify more strongly with each other than those in other departments pursuing different ends.

It doesn't take much for division—what we call "groupishness"—to appear. You could put 50 strangers in a room and randomly hand out 25 green t-shirts and 25 yellow t-shirts. In a hot minute, people will orient themselves into "Team Green" versus "Team Yellow." We can't help ourselves. We just do it.

This is just one simple example. The prevalence of this dynamic is huge.

Tribalism and groupishness are parts of our "inner chimp" defending the territory. Human nature is adapted to what enabled our ancestors to survive. Sometimes, that nature influences our behaviors in ways that create intra-organizational conflict. You can count on it.

Another example is when we try to treat everyone exactly the same and are surprised that different people respond differently to the same stimulus. How could that be? This occurs when we assume that everyone else should respond the way *we* respond to something.

Say you are a deeply empathic person. It's a beautiful part of what makes you a great person and is a major tool in your toolkit when encountering interpersonal challenges. You determine that the solution to an organizational problem would be if more people were just more empathetic. From there, you might design incentives and requirements for people to be more like you. You can see how this might not turn out how you'd hope, right?

People are different from each other, and because of our pre-wiring, we come by these differences honestly.

One more common error, perhaps the most egregious, is when managers treat their team members only as order-takers. Humans will comply if there are sufficient consequences for not complying and no good alternatives. But make no mistake: Humans aren't designed to just comply without context, questions, and brains of their own. Humans are whole beings with motivations, observations, and opinions.

A better way to lead real humans is to treat leadership as a dialogue—to be clear, a two-way dialogue. Sure, that's harder than just *telling*, but human nature isn't what we wish it were.

What if you could design your organization in a way that accounts for people being human? Really human, in the way that humans really are—not the idealized pawns in our utopian visions of homogeneity, compliant automatons, and an absence of groupishness.

Building an awareness of human nature into our organizational practices is possible. But you have to think differently. What opportunities are there for you to think differently about the people in your organization?

PEOPLE ENERGY PRINCIPLES
36 REFRAMES TO SHIFT HOW YOU THINK ABOUT PEOPLE & BUSINESS
NOTICE WHAT PEOPLE SAY AND BELIEVE WHAT PEOPLE DO.

6 NOTICE WHAT PEOPLE SAY AND BELIEVE WHAT PEOPLE DO.

You hear about walking one's talk. There's a reason we must try to behave according to our words: Our actions tell the true story.

Yet we're sometimes duped by peoples' words. Why is that?

It's a shortcut to believe someone's words. It takes less energy and allows us to focus on other things that clamor for our attention. But we should take care that we don't stop paying attention and don't write off a disconnect between words and deeds with a wave of the hand and a string of rationalizations. Maybe it's a one-off fluke, so we shouldn't jump to conclusions. Or maybe it's a signal that we pay closer attention to what someone is doing to get a clearer sense of what they truly believe.

How do you feel when you notice a difference between what someone says and does?

For example, a team member nods and agrees that they will do the task as you recommend. However, they don't complete the task. Alternatively, a business owner says that growing their business is important to her. Nonetheless, she makes decisions that don't enable growth.

It's frustrating when confronting such contradictions!

It can be hard to know what beliefs lie in others' hearts. So we should believe people's actions. Their actions tell us what they think and are the best predictors of what they'll do today and in the future.

When we believe actions and respond accordingly, it's less stressful because we don't put ourselves in the role of mind reader. We just pay attention to people's actions. What do you notice when you do this?

7 CHANGE PEOPLE BY ASSUMING PEOPLE CAN'T CHANGE.

Do you believe you can change people? Are you able to change what they are like and how they behave? How about vice versa? How much do you believe other people can change you? We usually are less generous with our estimates in response to that last question.

What happens when you sense that someone is trying to change you? How do you react? Usually, most of us will react with resistance. If you would resist being "changed," then what makes you think your colleagues would be any different?

Here's a weird trick. First, assume the person is who they are. They aren't going to change. But you need them to act differently when certain things happen. How do you accomplish that?

You start by adjusting the systems and incentives that influence these actions because we can always change a system even when we can't change a human.

When we change a system to more optimally influence each team member, the person typically behaves differently. They didn't change who they are, but they changed their behavior—all because you didn't try to change them—just the stuff around them. And that really matters.

PEOPLE ENERGY PRINCIPLES
36 REFRAMES TO SHIFT HOW YOU THINK ABOUT PEOPLE & BUSINESS
EVERY HUMAN IS UNIQUELY WIRED FOR SOMETHING. IT'S USEFUL TO FIGURE OUT WHAT THAT IS.

8 EVERY HUMAN IS UNIQUELY WIRED FOR SOMETHING. IT'S USEFUL TO FIGURE OUT WHAT THAT IS.

What's your superpower? Have you ever been asked that question? Have you ever asked yourself that question? You will talk about the talents you are best wired to show. Those are your superpowers.

Each of us is a little different when it comes to these talents.

Some people are good at many things, while others are good at just a few. But everyone has something special about how their skills, interests, and experiences come together, giving them a "superpower." This superpower informs and shapes their life purpose and how they want to invest their energy.

Here is a twist on this idea. The superpower doesn't have to be a narrow skill that happens to be world-class. Only the rare human is world-class at something. A superpower can be what Scott Adams calls a "talent stack."[1] A talent stack is a particular set of abilities that collectively create a unique capacity that calls on those talents to combine. We each have different talent stacks.

We are each uniquely wired for something.

This brings us to the main point of the principle. It's worth paying attention to the unique wiring of each team member, including you. It's being mindful about overlapping the accountabilities of a role with that unique wiring as much as is feasible.

What would look different in your organization if you did that?

---

[1] Adams, Scott. *How to Fail at Almost Everything and Still Win Big*. Scott Adams, Inc., 2023.

9 PEOPLE DO THINGS FOR REASONS, BUT NOT ALWAYS THE REASONS THEY GIVE YOU.

Have you ever been puzzled about why someone does (or does not do) something they claim to want to do? Our logical brains are designed to summon reasons for doing what we're doing and to figure out why we've decided what we've decided.

Yet, our logical brains tend to be overconfident in our ability to see the truth.

This isn't to say that these reasons we come up with are all wrong. They might be part of the story. Perhaps. But we often do things for reasons that run through us, like hidden, underground rivers. Those hidden reasons stir us, like the tectonic plates shifting the lands, rivers, and mountains of the earth.

These reasons are so hidden that we have forgotten they even are there.

We forget them for lots of reasons. Perhaps we established those reasons so long ago that there are layers of rationalization stacked on top of them. Maybe it's a little embarrassing to admit what is driving us. Perhaps there are so many intertwined reasons that it's impossible to sort out what's pushing and pulling us here and there.

It's hard to know the truth about why we do things; when we ask someone else why they've done something, they may be equally stymied. Sure, it's better to sound confident when we state our (partial) reasons. In fact, we often *feel* confident about the reasons we give. Really confident.

So when you notice people doing things and want to understand why, it's a good idea to ask them. Of course, ask when it's feasible to do so. But don't stop there and assume the reason given is the full story. There's often an emotional undercurrent also at work. Keep that in mind when you decide your next steps.

People do things for reasons, but not always (or only) the reasons they give you.

PEOPLE ENERGY PRINCIPLES
36 REFRAMES TO SHIFT HOW YOU THINK ABOUT PEOPLE & BUSINESS
BE CURIOUS. SHARE THE GROWTH MINDSET.

10 BE CURIOUS.
SHARE THE GROWTH MINDSET.

What separates the disruptors from the dinosaurs in the business jungle? Simple. It's all about mindset. Picture this: A company where everyone's hungry for growth, constantly probing, tinkering, and learning. That's the growth mindset in action.[1] In a world where change is the only constant, staying curious is like having a superpower.

Curiosity is the engine that drives innovation and keeps the competition eating your dust.

Now, a different take: Imagine a team stuck in its ways, clinging to what it knows like a security blanket. That's a fixed mindset: fixed, as in not open to evolution, and fixed, as in insistent that the current methods are the best every time. No matter what else changes around us.

When you're too busy patting yourself on the back, there's no room for bold moves or breakthroughs. Innovation? Forget about it. You're too busy guarding your precious status quo. Is that what you want?

Let's talk about motivation.

With a growth mindset, every setback is just a chance to be the hero in your success story. It's like having a personal cheerleader in your brain, pushing you to tackle challenges head-on. Do we experience failure? Sure, but it's just a pitstop on the road to greatness. That's the fuel that keeps the team's performance burning bright. If you want to soar with the eagles, ditch the fixed mindset and embrace the power of the growth mindset.

What proportion of your team adheres to the growth mindset? Find ways to increase that percentage just a little and reap the benefits. And remember to stay curious. Curious is open. Open can evolve, while fixed mindsets are sticks in the mud.

You share a powerful mindset when you disseminate a culture of growth and curiosity. Be curious today and every day. Share the growth mindset.

---

[1] Carol S. Dweck. *Mindset*. Ballantine Books, 2006.

11 EVERY SOLUTION IS FIRST A HYPOTHESIS. REALITY TEST.

Scientific rigor isn't about the subject you are researching. Oftentimes, we see scientific terminology used without applying the procedural rigor to back it up. For example, some (not all) uses of neuro, science, and research-based might be making stronger cases than the data can support. It's an understandable error—doing science well is hard.

What makes for scientific rigor when trying to understand reality?

One of the most important parts of scientific rigor is the patience and humility to realize that our first thoughts on a solution to a problem could be completely wrong. The realization that our solution is, first and foremost, a *hypothesis*.

A hypothesis is a tentative explanation for an observation, phenomenon, or scientific problem that can be tested by further investigation. It's something that's taken to be true for argument or investigation, an assumption.

A hypothesis *might* be true. Or it might *not*.

So often, when we first imagine a solution, our brains want to lock into that solution. It's more comforting to be certain than it is to be open to being wrong. To accomplish this, we look for confirming evidence and ignore contrary indicators. Ironically, this tendency leads to being wrong more often.

Have you got the picture?

Now, imagine what happens when several people have different opinions (hypotheses) about the best solution. Each person is inclined to lock into their own solution, which then creates conflict. The arguments center on why each opinion is right. Conflict ensues. Heels dig in. Trust drops.

What happens if, instead, each of these people proposes their solution as a hypothesis—a hypothesis that very well could be shown to be wrong? The shared commitment to finding the truth becomes the center of the problem-solving arena rather than an argument over who "has it right." The group can focus on finding ways to test hypotheses and share their creative energy.

Be more scientific. Treat your solution like a hypothesis.

REALITY TEST

PEOPLE ENERGY PRINCIPLES
36 REFRAMES TO SHIFT HOW YOU THINK ABOUT PEOPLE & BUSINESS
REAL SKIN IN THE GAME CREATES TRUE ACCOUNTABILITY.

12 REAL SKIN IN THE GAME CREATES TRUE ACCOUNTABILITY.

What is "skin in the game"? If you are in sales, you might recognize this phrase as referring to eligibility for a commission or performance bonus. This is part, but not ALL, of what I'm talking about. In his book "Skin in the Game," Nassim Taleb establishes this principle more broadly.[1]

Taleb asserts that true skin in the game means both benefiting from the rewards of decisions and exposure to the consequences of your choices. Even consequences that you couldn't have anticipated. So you don't just get the upside when you win; you're also exposed to what goes wrong due to your decisions and work.

Here's a thought experiment: Imagine you're building a bridge for village townspeople. Now imagine the village king telling you that if the bridge fails, if people are hurt or die, the same fate awaits you. That's real skin in the game—visceral skin in the game. You would then aim to build a very secure and awesome bridge, wouldn't you? You would make such a bridge even if it takes more time to build it more securely and requires more expensive materials.

Now, suppose you are a traveling bridge maker who scoots from village to village building fast and cheap bridges. To be fair, you are experienced at bridge building, so you should be good at it, right?

But you can't be found if you are 150 miles away when your bridge fails. You gain the payment for building a bridge but are exposed to no downside if the bridge fails. That is the absence of skin in the game.

Now, apply that to an organization's policy setting. Let's say an administrator decides it would make his job easier if everyone restricted their materials acquisition method to using one form submitted only on Mondays and Wednesdays. This system helps the administrator's workflow tremendously! He is more efficient and can better balance the multiple components of his role, so this is obviously an improvement. Right? His efficiency metrics are way better, so it must be right.

But it's wrong because this change negatively impacts many other organizational roles. These changes make it harder for the operations staff to succeed because they can't always acquire the necessary materials to meet their success metrics. The administrator, meanwhile, experiences none of the negative consequences that the operations staff experiences. Imagine how much better this could have gone if the administrator had talked to the people impacted by the process change: The people with skin in the game regarding materials availability. That would have been better.

Another example: Sometimes, we believe things would work better in theory if we did things a particular way. Maybe we read about it in a book, or a consultant recommends it. Perhaps we are eliminating an organizational layer or functional area that doesn't fit the ideal model. So we talk the executive suite into doing things the new-fangled way the books tell us is the perfect way.

But we don't bother talking to the people who will have to do things differently if we make such changes. We haven't found out the purpose of the activities that don't fit into the ideal model. We assume we know best without checking with the people with skin in the game.

This doesn't mean we can't make changes. Far from it! It just alerts us to the importance of checking with the people the changes will impact. It reminds us that people do things a certain way for reasons. Maybe it's not a good reason, or perhaps it is, but you won't know until you check your assumptions by asking those with skin in the game.

Always check. Don't assume. Whenever possible, make sure YOU have skin in the game for your decisions.

[1] Nassim Nicholas Taleb. *Skin in the Game.* Random House, 2020.

PEOPLE ENERGY PRINCIPLES
36 REFRAMES TO SHIFT HOW YOU THINK ABOUT PEOPLE & BUSINESS
PERSONALITY CONFLICTS AREN'T ABOUT PERSONALITY, THEY'RE ORGANIZATIONAL CLARITY PROBLEMS.

13 PERSONALITY CONFLICTS AREN'T ABOUT PERSONALITY, THEY'RE ORGANIZATIONAL CLARITY PROBLEMS.

What if I told you that workplace personality conflicts are often just symptoms of operational clarity problems? Here's the truth: I've never encountered a personality conflict that wasn't rooted in deeper issues of organizational clarity.

What may appear as a clash of personalities is often just the tip of the iceberg. It's the visible surface-level manifestation of more significant problems lurking beneath. The real cause lies in ambiguity surrounding roles and decision-making authority.

Imagine this scenario: Two individuals each believe they have the power to make a particular decision, but they disagree. It sparks conflict, right? Well, it's not their personalities at odds—it's the lack of clarity about who holds the authority. Another common clarity issue is when no one takes ownership of a decision, leading to a blame game and a lack of accountability.

Of course, it doesn't stop there.

Misaligned incentives and accountability can also fuel conflicts. Picture a situation where someone's performance metrics depend not only on their own work but also on their colleagues' actions. If they have no authority or means to influence their colleagues, tensions arise. Different incentives and responsibilities create a breeding ground for conflict.

Now, let's consider the case of someone promoted to a managerial role without the necessary skills or support. They're suddenly tasked with managing their former peers, feeling overwhelmed and ill-prepared. It's a recipe for conflict, with personality clashes often masquerading as the root cause.

Personality conflicts are merely the visible surface, painting the tone of the conflict. But it's the lack of organizational clarity that fuels the discord beneath. So, instead of solely addressing the personalities involved, we must dive deeper, resolve clarity issues, redefine roles, provide proper training and support, and align incentives and accountability.

By doing so, we can transform personality conflicts into opportunities for growth, collaboration, and productivity within the organization. It's time to tackle the underlying clarity problems head-on and pave the way for a more harmonious and effective work environment.

Remember, we can't change people's personalities, but we can improve operational clarity. Personality conflicts aren't about personality.

14 APPLY THE TRUST ALGORITHM: ACCOUNTABILITY = AUTHORITY = CAPABILITY.

In the last principle, we highlight how so-called personality conflicts stem from a lack of operational clarity and coherence. To refresh the point, when two people have different assumptions about who's in charge of this or that decision, their assumptions spark conflict. That's just one example of how a lack of operational clarity and coherence can create interpersonal dysfunction.

But there are more ways things can go awry.

The best way to describe organizational coherence is through **The Trust Algorithm**. What does trust have to do with organizational clarity, coherence, and reducing conflict? The more your organization enhances trust between the people involved, the less frequently you will find unproductive conflict. In fact, the more trust, the better the likelihood you can have productive conflicts that generate new ideas and better, clearer views of the situation.

There are many books, podcasts, and webinars about creating trust: Most trust-building advice centers on interpersonal interaction and communication tactics. Be more open, ask more questions, seek to understand before being understood, etc. This is all excellent advice.

But that's not what The Trust Algorithm is about.

The Trust Algorithm points to how an organizational structure, if done properly, can set the stage for trust. When The Trust Algorithm is adhered to, it's like swimming with the current. When there's a misalignment in The Trust Algorithm components, it's like swimming upstream and against the current. Wouldn't you prefer to have an organization that made building a high-trust culture easier?

Explaining The Trust Algorithm.

The Trust Algorithm describes the variables that generate unnecessary conflict and reduce team trust if they get out of whack. These variables must be synced up and balanced to get the kind of operational coherence and trust that makes high performance far more likely to be achieved. Here are the three variables that are part of The Trust Algorithm:

ACCOUNTABILITY = AUTHORITY = CAPABILITY

A more detailed description of The Trust Algorithm can be found in the Appendix, but I will briefly overview it here. The three parts of The Trust Algorithm are defined as follows:

- Accountability — The responsibility for one's actions and decisions, including exposure to positive and negative consequences.

- Authority — The legitimate power vested in a person by their role to expend material, technical, financial, and human resources. Illegitimate power is not authority—it's manipulation.

- Capability — The ability to do required work and a function of having the necessary knowledge, skills, mental computing power, and interest or willingness.

The algorithm sets up these three variables with an equal sign (=) between them. That means greater trust exists when each of these is balanced equally for each person in each seat. When one or more of these variables is NOT equal to the other variables, conflict and dysfunction become more likely, just like in the examples provided at the beginning of this section.

Expected types of dysfunctions arise from different sorts of imbalances between two variables. If you'd like to learn more about each of the patterns of dysfunction that occur from each type of The Trust Algorithm imbalance, there's a full description in the Appendix.

Consider your organization. Where are there disconnects in The Trust Algorithm? If you were to ask around, what do you think you would find? Apply The Trust Algorithm, and trust and high performance get easier.

PEOPLE ENERGY PRINCIPLES
36 REFRAMES TO SHIFT HOW YOU THINK ABOUT PEOPLE & BUSINESS
WORK HARD TO MAKE THINGS (MORE) SIMPLE.

5 WORK HARD TO MAKE THINGS (MORE) SIMPLE.

Complicated is easy. Simple is hard.

What!? That doesn't sound right. But maybe it is. Consider the quote, "Pardon the length of my letter, as I didn't have the time to make it shorter." There's truth in that, isn't there?

When I say simple, I'm not talking about simplistic—not watering something down so much that you lose the fidelity and context of the situation. There's a kind of simplicity that holds a LOT of information. This simplicity points to meta-patterns that are larger than the problems at hand. That's the simplicity you want to seek; teasing it out is hard work. But boy, is it ever worth it!

"We cannot solve our problems with the same level of thinking that created them."
—Albert Einstein.

An example is how we think about the role of a manager. Many managers were trained with the expectation that their job is to ensure high-quality, highly efficient operations. Which it is. But not ONLY that.

More recently, managers have also been expected to learn coaching skills, empathy, and various techniques that seemingly reduce the efficiency of the operation. I frequently talk to leaders about how to help managers learn these skills and figure out when to empathize and when to hold the employee accountable. Gosh, it's gotten so complicated to navigate all of these competing priorities!

How do we simplify this?

One way is to reframe a manager's job as being accountable for boosting the performance of the collective team. Coaching, empathizing, and providing clear, constructive feedback all work together to maximize team performance. That's the point—a simpler way to think about it.

"Truth is ever to be found in the simplicity, and not in the multiplicity and confusion of things." —Isaac Newton

Simplification is explaining something complex in understandable words.

If you must rely on abstruse vernacular and incoherent reasoning, you don't quite understand what you're trying to say. Don't do what I just did—instead, use real-people words.

If the best you can do is string together a bunch of $20 words, like "abstruse" and "vernacular," you may only think you understand your point—but you don't yet. Keep working at it. If you can explain what you mean to a 6-year-old and they "get it," then you are on to something.

Here's an excerpt from a Sherlock Holmes story that illustrates two perspectives of one situation — one meaninglessly complex and the other simple and directly on point.

Sherlock Holmes and Dr. Watson are on a camping trip. In the middle of the night, Holmes wakes up and gives Dr. Watson a nudge.

"Watson," he says, "look up in the sky and tell me what you see."

"I see millions of stars, Holmes," says Watson.

"And what do you conclude from that, Watson?"

Watson thinks for a moment. "Well," he says, "astronomically, it tells me that there are millions of galaxies and potentially billions of planets. Astrologically, I observe that Saturn is in Leo. Horologically, I deduce that the time is approximately a quarter past three. Meteorologically, I suspect that we will have a beautiful day tomorrow. Theologically, I see that God is all-powerful, and we are small and insignificant. Uh, what does it tell you, Holmes?"

"Watson, you idiot! Someone has stolen our tent!"

Listen to the feedback from people telling you what's unclear about your explanation. Ask if you are making sense. Listen and take on what they tell you. It's hard work, this simplicity.

"That's been one of my mantras—focus and simplicity. Simple can be harder than complex: You have to work hard to get your thinking clean to make it simple. But it's worth it in the end because once you get there, you can move mountains."
— Steve Jobs

It may be comforting to know that some of the greatest minds who are quoted in this chapter have sought simplicity. It's hard. That's why when you work hard to make hard things more simple, you'll know it's worth the effort!

PEOPLE ENERGY PRINCIPLES
36 REFRAMES TO SHIFT HOW YOU THINK ABOUT PEOPLE & BUSINESS
TRUST COMES AFTER COOPERATION. IN THAT ORDER.

16 TRUST COMES AFTER COOPERATION. IN THAT ORDER.

We frequently believe we'll cooperate once someone or some party has shown themselves trustworthy. It makes good sense, doesn't it? Why trust someone who hasn't demonstrated trustworthiness?

You'll probably be surprised to learn, as I was, that this isn't actually how trust works.

Years ago, I read Robert Axelrod's "The Evolution of Cooperation."[1] He's a game theorist who ran many simulations of cooperation strategies in a "prisoner's dilemma" situation. That means that an individual can gain the most in the short term by taking advantage of the other party, but when both parties gain, things are better for everyone in the long run. Further, he explored how cooperation emerges without prior trust, even in the strangest circumstances.

A striking example was the fighting parties in WWI trench warfare. Sometimes, the fighting stopped, and the opposing forces began to behave cooperatively. As they tentatively cooperated, this led to more cooperation and eventually increased trust. That is until the bigwigs forced them to start fighting again.

This pattern suggests that if we want to build a trusting relationship, we won't get there through logical argument or bragging about our credentials. Instead, we ought to find ways to first demonstrate trust by being cooperative.

Could we be taken advantage of if we do that? Yes, perhaps, but it's much less likely than you think. And if the occasional person takes advantage, but the net gain is much more trust across all your relationships, so what? It seems like the strategically wise trade-off is to exercise a little vulnerability because it pays off over a longer timespan.

Remember: Trust comes after cooperation, in that order.

[1] Axelrod, Robert. *The Evolution of Cooperation*. Basic Books, 2009.

PEOPLE ENERGY PRINCIPLES
36 REFRAMES TO SHIFT HOW YOU THINK ABOUT PEOPLE & BUSINESS
DECISIONS GO WHERE THEY BELONG.

17 DECISIONS GO WHERE THEY BELONG.

Decision-making should be driven by those who have genuine accountability for the outcomes—true accountability is the answer. It's not about assigning blame; it's about taking ownership and being responsible for the positive and negative consequences.

Accountability becomes elusive when decisions don't consider the input of those directly affected. Take customer service standards, for example. If the CEO decides on standards without consulting the frontline staff interacting with customers daily, there's a lack of accountability. Their valuable insights are essential to making informed decisions.

Collaborative decisions that involve multiple departments require someone who can effectively coordinate and take responsibility. Simply delegating decision-making to one department head may lead to narrow perspectives and missed opportunities for optimization. A broader view, encompassing all relevant areas, ensures decisions benefit the entire organization.

Decisions belong to those who understand the impact, possess the authority, and are accountable for the outcomes. They actively involve the right people, seek diverse perspectives, and make informed choices that propel the organization forward.

Imagine how much team performance you can unlock if decision-making goes where it belongs: In the hands of accountable individuals who consider the consequences, involve the right stakeholders, and make decisions with integrity. By embracing accountability, we pave the way for effective and impactful decision-making.

Be mindful that decisions go where they belong.

18 COMMUNICATION IS MORE THAN SAYING WORDS.

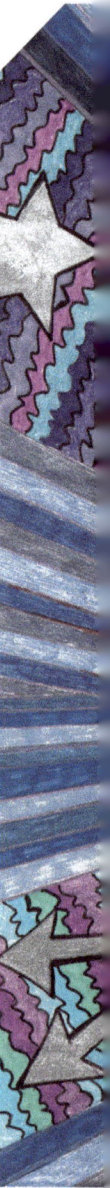

Communication isn't just about words; we all know it's more than that, right?

Imagine you're on a sales call, eager to understand the product being pitched to you and your team. You start asking questions, seeking clarity on how it works and its relevance to your specific needs. However, the salesperson becomes frustrated, thrown off their rhythm and script. Their focus is solely on delivering their pitch, not making sure you understand.

How do you think your team felt? Not great. And not too enthused about buying anything from that salesperson.

See, good communication goes beyond simply delivering a message. It's about ensuring that the receiver understands your intended message. There's a whole world of non-verbal communication to consider. We use body movements, micro-expressions, sound volume, tone, and many other nuances to get our point across.

It's about engaging in an exchange, a discussion back and forth. It's about being mindful of your body language, how you present yourself on video calls, your postures, and the messages they convey. Are you genuinely interested? Do your facial expressions show attentiveness? If you're video camera is off, how would you know?

Communication is so much more than a string of words. It's the little things that truly matter.

So, the next time you communicate, remember that words are just the tip of the iceberg. We communicate more effectively if we pay attention to the non-verbal cues, create meaningful exchanges, and ensure our message resonates with those on the receiving end.

Communication is more than saying words.

PEOPLE ENERGY PRINCIPLES
36 REFRAMES TO SHIFT HOW YOU THINK ABOUT PEOPLE & BUSINESS
START WHERE THE OTHER PERSON IS.

19 START WHERE THE OTHER PERSON IS.

We all start where we are. We can't help it. Our thoughts, views, and assumptions about what's right, wrong, and true color our starting point in any dialogue. When we seek to influence others, we unknowingly frame our arguments through these filters.

But consider those we're seeking to influence. Where do you suppose they are starting from? From where *they* are. Their ability to hear and understand is filtered through their thoughts, views, and assumptions about what's right, wrong, and true.

So what's your aim? Is it to force the other person to agree to something they might not fully understand, or is it to shift and broaden the other party's perspective to better see where you are coming from? Is it more important to be told you are right, or is it more important to be understood and influential?

Start where the other person is.

20 CO-AUTHOR: MORE MINDS, MORE BETTER.

Is it better to make a decision in isolation that impacts lots of things and people? Or is it better to gather perspectives from other people before setting a course of action?

Problems that deal with people tend to be complex. Such issues are more complicated and multifaceted than we imagine through our limited view because people are different. We're each uniquely wired so that we will see things differently. We prize different things.

Therefore, wouldn't it be wise to, at the very least, ask a few people to weigh in who are looking at the situation through different portals? It's still your decision to make. Think how your extended advisory squad feels about your choices, knowing they have been consulted. Think how much better your decisions will be in quality.

Diversity matters.

You might think that involving more people means trying to gain consensus. That "more minds" means more different people who have to agree before anything gets done. No, no, no. To believe that, you must either default to the echo chamber of your single mind or give up your decision-making authority to the group. This is a false dichotomy.

Gather perspectives, not votes.

If a particular decision needs all the players to have an equal vote, that would be your choice to apply that decision-making method. However, it's not your only option for greater inclusivity in your decision-making process.

Perhaps you are concerned that if you get another person's opinions on something and take a contrary approach, they'll be unhappy with you because you didn't follow their advice. Pro tip–they'd be more unhappy with you if you hadn't bothered to ask them at all. How so? Because when you don't ask, you demonstrate that you don't care what others think and don't believe they have anything useful to offer.

Which outcome would make *you* more unhappy— someone making a decision opposite to your opinion after consulting with you or the same decision being made after not asking you at all?

What if you aren't the one with the authority to decide? If you don't have decision authority for an area or set of areas, you could raise the flag and encourage others to pull in "more minds." You don't always have to be the decider to leverage this principle.

More minds, more better. Win-win.

PEOPLE ENERGY PRINCIPLES
36 REFRAMES TO SHIFT HOW YOU THINK ABOUT PEOPLE & BUSINESS
DON'T GET STUCK ADDRESSING SYMPTOMS.

21 DON'T GET STUCK ADDRESSING SYMPTOMS.

Problem. Solution! Problem. Solution! We are acting fast, which is what we want, right?

BUT … oh, no! These are the same problems over and over again!

Does it ever feel that way when working through "people problems" in your organization? It's a common challenge. There is just so much to do in a typical organization, and having a fast reaction time to common problems is a winning move—usually.

What happens when we notice that we might be sacrificing the chance to solve a deeper issue so that we see less of this "common problem" we've come to expect over and over? What are your most common problems? Are they symptoms of a deeper issue? How would you know?

This is where bringing several teammates and experts together to work through key issues can bear fruit. Often, solving a problem at the root cause can unlock more capabilities and growth in your team. Imagine what that might feel like!

The hard part can be making time to do this. Actually, the really hard part is having the vulnerability to admit you (we) don't have all of the answers. Hard things like this are worth it, though.

It brings to mind the truism that once we see something we didn't notice before, we can't "unsee" it. If you're like me, you wonder how you could have missed that thing for so long when it seems so obvious now.

But we do miss things, and we'll miss more stuff as we go.

So we can be diligent about not getting stuck resolving symptoms and create a discipline for discovering root causes that unlock growth and capability. Don't get stuck addressing symptoms.

22 SMALLEST CHANGES FOR THE BIGGEST IMPACTS.

Do you want to be innovative? Really innovative? We hear successful innovators talk about failing fast, which sounds worse than it is. They really mean to take smart bets that, if you're wrong, don't take you out of the game.

It's not about crashing and burning; it's about making calculated moves. Think of it like placing some, but not all, of your chips on the table, knowing you won't lose your shirt if luck's not on your side.

Enter the principle: Smallest changes for biggest impacts. We're talking about making moves that pack a punch without blowing up your whole operation. Smart bets. It's like nudging the domino that sets off a chain reaction rather than trying to topple the whole line in one go.

Smart, small changes are your secret weapon. Finding small things that make a big difference are your baby steps leading you toward progress without getting out over your skis. Sure, have a plan, but…

> *"Everybody has a plan until they get*
> *punched in the mouth."*
> —*Mike Tyson*

Forget about crafting some grand master plan that's as fragile as a house of cards. That's a recipe for disaster. Instead, focus on making small tweaks, testing the waters, and adjusting the course as you go.

Why? Small changes are less risky. They're like dipping your toe in the water before diving headfirst into the deep end. You're not betting the farm on a wild idea; you're making calculated moves that inch you closer to your goals.

Next time you're itching to shake things up, remember it's not about swinging for the fences. It's about making the smallest changes for the biggest impacts. That's how the game changers play it. It's a winning strategy.

PEOPLE ENERGY PRINCIPLES
36 REFRAMES TO SHIFT HOW YOU THINK ABOUT PEOPLE & BUSINESS
DIAGNOSE BEFORE YOU PRESCRIBE.

23 DIAGNOSE
BEFORE YOU PRESCRIBE.

Just because you can quickly visualize a solution doesn't mean you should act on it. ~~Even~~ especially if you're smart because smart people are really, really good at fooling themselves.

If you jump to a particular solution or prescription, you will find it harder to notice details about the situation that warrant a different solution—or an additional one. This is because you are a human, and humans are subject to confirmation bias.

When you pause to diagnose, you might also describe more than your first guess at the root causes. Doing this helps clarify the issue and the criteria for a good solution. Then, work through as many alternative solutions as you can imagine. If you can't imagine anything else, ask other people to help you come up with different perspectives and solutions. Then, test your solution before you scale it.

Diagnose, then prescribe.

24 PROMPT GRASSROOTS DECISION-MAKING OFTEN.

People tend to think that hierarchies run only top-down. That's wrong. And ill-considered, to be blunt about it. Hierarchies can also bloom upward and outward if only you let them.

Imagine a culture where the best ideas flow up and across your team. What would be different if everyone's mental default is no longer always going "upward" for answers? What if people's default setting is to seek input laterally and from the frontline before asking up the chain?

For example, you might discover that problems with delivery times aren't caused by a lack of accountability that needs to be admonished and corrected. Instead, they result from a change in customer behavior on the front lines, an issue with the technology used by your customer-facing team, or something else that points to a new service opportunity.

Or perhaps you'd like to see people innovate more and develop ideas independently, instead of waiting for the ideas to trickle down to them. Do the people on your team believe they have the autonomy to suggest and implement improvements? Are you sure? When you cultivate a culture of innovation and independence on the front lines, you might be surprised at what magic people create.

Magic is what you get when you prompt more grassroots decision-making.

Like many business leaders, you may feel like you've got to drive and steer everything.Every priority. Every initiative. All decisions need to be associated with near-term actions. Instead, what if we plant "idea seeds" for the future without pushing for immediate action? Water and till the soil and see what comes of it!

Envision your role as a seed planter and good-idea waterer instead of the genius who comes up with all the ideas yourself. First, do it purposefully. Eventually, it will become a habit, and you'll do it automatically.

In what ways are you tilling the ground? What kinds of idea seeds are you planting? Are you planting enough seeds so we are still harvesting a bounty when poor weather prevents some ideas from growing and bearing fruit?

A healthy culture of ownership and innovation ensures that grassroots decision-making works. Your efforts will pay off. They will! We just don't know which ones or when. But we know that planting seeds and sharing the burden with others puts us all in the best position to win together over the long run.

Grassroots decision-making must be cultivated. It may not have the immediate satisfaction of summoning the troops, calling to arms, and sounding the battle trumpet. But that's ok. If you plant seeds, water them with faith in your team's capabilities, and shine on them with the sunlight of values and purpose, you'll be amazed at what grows.

PEOPLE ENERGY PRINCIPLES
36 REFRAMES TO SHIFT HOW YOU THINK ABOUT PEOPLE & BUSINESS
SOMETIMES THERE'S ONE RIGHT WAY. PROBABLY NOT THIS TIME.

25 SOMETIMES THERE'S ONE RIGHT WAY. PROBABLY NOT THIS TIME.

You have a complex, difficult problem involving people, teams, and competing priorities. The situation keeps evolving, and each party has a different opinion about what should happen. Maybe you're looking for the best compensation strategy for your new sales hires, trying to find the best way to recruit and interview people for your team, or you just want a process that smooths out the interactions between production and sales.

What's the right way to deal with the situation at hand?

It's tempting to find out the "best practice" for solving your problem. But that presumes that your situation is just like every other situation—the people are the same, the business is the same, and the point where your business is in its lifecycle is the same. Regarding complex issues, what works over there may not work over here. Or, perhaps, what worked before won't work now.

Best practices aren't always the best.

- Sometimes, best practices are great and just what you need when the situation is straightforward.

- Sometimes, best practices are a good starting point that you can tweak where needed when you see how it works.

- Sometimes, unfortunately, a best practice is just the old way of doing things at a mediocre level and not living up to its reputation as "best" anymore.

How do we know what to do if there's more than one right way to do things?

We start with questions to better understand the situation: What are you solving for—maximum profits, customer experience, or a great culture? What values are you prioritizing as most important? Are you maximizing those values, trying to level-set them to a proper point, or looking to change the volatility of those values? What time horizon are you looking for results—this week, next quarter, or within two years? What are you willing to sacrifice to get these results?

Those are a bunch of really hard questions!

Let's say that you can answer those questions. Let's also say you are ready to make a sound decision on what to do as a result. Now I ask, would the people affected by your judgments answer those questions differently?

Complex situations are hard to manage, but you must do your best in a leadership role. If you are the decider for this situation, you must decide. Or not decide, which is also a decision and could very well be a viable option if waiting it out could crystalize the situation.

You don't have to think it through alone.

Some of the best leaders I've worked with will say, "I like to get input from at least three well-informed people with different kinds of expertise and then triangulate." Also, "I feel more confident in my decisions when I have different people to work through the issue with." These leaders have learned that by listening and considering input from various perspectives, their blind spots shrink. When blind spots shrink, the chance of making an intractable error decreases. When blind spots shrink, we can better decide whether a best practice is best for this situation—or not.

One consideration when taking advice from experts:

Don't unthinkingly follow the advice of experts without understanding what you are deciding and what you are sacrificing in the wake of that decision. Sometimes experts suggest things that, if they don't work out for you, don't hurt them. Said differently, those experts don't have "skin in the game" when solving your problem. They don't experience the direct consequences of a poorly considered decision. When people don't have skin in the game, they are inclined to be overconfident about riskier options.

There's no compelling correction mechanism that changes an expert's advice. The theory continues to look good, and their careers improve if their advice is consistently "correct," whether or not it works for you. YOU are the only one who can aptly test whether something works for you and your situation. So, gather ideas and test things out. A great way to use experts is to get insights from their exposure to a variety of similar situations and help you identify multiple ways to solve a problem. This matters because sometimes there's one right answer, but that's rare.

Remember, sometimes there's one right way, but probably not this time.

26   FEEL STUCK?
EXTEND YOUR TIME HORIZON, THE VIEW IS DIFFERENT

Have you ever felt super frustrated? Stuck? So bad you can't get past a barrier stopping you from something important. So vexing it's also preventing you from focusing on other important things in business and life. It's a common problem we all encounter from time to time.

If you are like me, here's how it often goes.

> *Ugh! If I can't get this thing working right by the end of the week, I will have these other problems next week. That's yucky and bugging me. I want things to go smoothly and efficiently, but it's not happening. Triple ugh!*

Is the sentiment familiar?

What if you could take a moment and consider the long-term goals related to what you are frustrated about? Instead of thinking about the inconveniences of next week if this week doesn't go as planned, think about where you want to be in 6 months or a year from now.

For example, our family has been working towards building a new home near my parents' house. It's a complex and lengthy process that began with getting a surveyor. To put it mildly, getting a surveyor in 2021 amid construction booms and staffing shortages was tough. It took nearly a year because neither my husband nor I had much extra time to repeatedly call when another surveying firm abandoned us for the umpteenth time.

Here's how I reframed it: I recalled that we wanted to be in the house before my son entered high school and, ideally, not go into heavy debt to pay for the process. This reminder meant we had time to wait for things to cool off. This reframing took the edge off the urgency and frustration, which was incredibly helpful.

This process is "extending your time horizon." Instead of fixating on a 1–2-week horizon, extend your timeline of intent further out. *Way* out.

You can also call this "gaining perspective." This is accurate, but I find it more helpful to consider my time horizon of concern. There are many ways to take a different perspective, but the time horizon takes you from reactivity and tactical madness to the open air of long-term vision.

Don't you feel like you can breathe easier with that reframe? I do. Try it out.

ARROW OF TIME

PEOPLE ENERGY PRINCIPLES
36 REFRAMES TO SHIFT HOW YOU THINK ABOUT PEOPLE & BUSINESS
WHAT WE KNOW FOR SURE IS TINY. BLIND SPOTS ARE MANY.

WHAT WE KNOW FOR SURE IS TINY.
BLIND SPOTS ARE MANY.

Are you a genius? No? Me either. Or maybe you are a genius.

Sure, maybe we're smarter than average, but none of us knows it all. None of us can know it all because we're just one human with one set of eyes and ears. It's impossible to know it all, no matter what other redeeming qualities we might have—intellectual and otherwise.

We have blind spots. Massive blind spots. All over the place. To make matters worse, we are massively blind to our massive blind spots, except when people point them out. Which we usually hate, although it's a gift to be told, if we can handle it.

Imagine a house. You can see a large, beautiful house with two floors, lovely cedar siding, a front and back entrance, and a dozen rooms. Now imagine that you can only look through one window to see this house—just one.

How much do you know about this house? How much can you see? How well-equipped are you to decide how to decorate a home you can only see the corner of?

When we look at our organization and the people of our organization, we are looking through one window. Just one window. It might be a narrow, tiny window or a nice, big skylight with a generous top-down view, but it's just one window. If you want to understand the house, you will want to get insights from other people looking through different windows.

Have you ever been surprised at how differently someone in your organization interprets something said or done? Or perhaps you've devised a solution to solve a problem you see, and your solution doesn't create the expected outcomes? It's possible you only looked through one window to see the house and missed some important information.

The truth is that no one can see through all the windows. We NEED other people and their different perspectives to help us all see better together. These perspectives help us see more of the house.

Here's an example:

Let's say you have several people in the same role but at different retail locations. The compensation for this role is a mixture of a base salary and commission. To move an experienced and skilled individual from an established location to a new location, you increase their base salary so they don't experience a reduction in total pay for making the move. From the view of that individual and the leaders involved in that decision, this decision seems like fair compensation.

Now, imagine another person in the same role hears through the grapevine that this person has a higher base salary than they do but doesn't know about the difference in commission opportunities. From their "window," it looks quite different and even unfair. Differing perspectives and limited access to full information are common issues in any organization.

Remembering that what we DON'T know *always* exceeds what we DO know can help us perceive a situation more accurately without jumping to as many conclusions or missing the chance to frame a decision in a way that more people will understand.

There's a lot we don't know in the world. In fact, the more we know about something, the more we see that there is a LOT MORE we don't know.

This pattern is so prevalent that we have a label for it—the Dunning-Kruger effect.[1] The effect asserts that most people are overconfident about their abilities, and the least competent and least informed people are the most overconfident. It's only when we truly know a lot, a whole lot, about something that we realize the depth of our ignorance.

[1] Contributors to Wikimedia projects. "Dunning–Kruger Effect - *Wikipedia*." Wikipedia, May 16, 2024. https://en.wikipedia.org/wiki/Dunning-Kruger_effect.

It's natural to assume we know. It's human nature. But there is so much we don't know.

This isn't new news. We can easily recognize what we know we know (known knowns) and what we know we don't know (known unknowns). But there are also unknown unknowns—the things we don't know we don't know. It's our unknown unknowns that can hijack us because we don't know where they are hiding until it becomes clear. When more unknown unknowns become known unknowns, then we are better positioned to make really good decisions.

"There are known knowns; there are things we know we know. We also know there are known unknowns; that is to say we know there are some things we do not know. But there are also unknown unknowns - the ones we don't know we don't know."
—Donald Rumsfeld

Don't get overconfident. Don't get complacent. Remember to stay curious.

28 MANAGER MEANS ACCOUNTABILITY FOR TEAM RESULTS.

Do you find yourself caught in the conflict between managers and leaders? People often argue that managers are bad due to their association with hierarchy, while leaders are celebrated as great and wonderful. But what if I told you that you can be both a manager and a leader, or even just one or the other, or none at all? And you can be good or bad at both, either one, or neither one.

Let's delve into the definition of manager specifically so we can clear the air.

As a manager, your responsibility is to ensure the purposeful work results of others. It's not about doing their work for them; it's about developing your team and equipping them with resources, tools, and support. You establish effective communication channels, answer their questions, and help them navigate different parts of the organization. Your goal is to enable your team's work results. And when someone isn't carrying their weight, you collaborate with them to find solutions. Is it a temporary setback, a solvable issue, or a need to reassess their responsibilities? It's essential to avoid prioritizing one person's needs at the expense of the entire team's ability to excel.

To thrive as a manager, it makes perfect sense to be employee-centered, training-oriented, and focused on development. After all, you are accountable for your team's work results. By striking the right balance between managerial and leadership qualities, you can steer your team toward success while fostering a supportive and productive work environment. So, are you ready to embrace the diverse aspects of being a manager and a leader?

Understanding what a manager is matters.

It's crucial because it gives you clarity and purpose when navigating your professional path. You become confident and competent. Effective management creates efficient work environments. It fosters strong teams, necessary resources, and open communication. Collaboration, productivity, and employee satisfaction thrive. Misconceptions and conflicts are prevented. You realize management is about leadership, guidance, and enabling others to achieve results. Harmonious relationships between managers and team members emerge. Organizations identify and develop talented individuals. Skills and qualities are honed for effective leadership. Training, mentorship, and professional development drive success.

In a nutshell, knowing what a manager is unleashes personal growth, positive work environments, conflict resolution, and effective leadership. It's fundamental. Embrace it.

Doing management well is a good and honorable thing.

PEOPLE ENERGY PRINCIPLES
36 REFRAMES TO SHIFT HOW YOU THINK ABOUT PEOPLE & BUSINESS
LEADERSHIP IS DEFINED BY THE PRESENCE OF FOLLOWERS.

29 LEADERSHIP IS DEFINED BY THE PRESENCE OF FOLLOWERS.

Have you ever wondered what leadership truly means? It's a topic that has gained immense popularity over the years. People tend to view leadership as something virtuous and inherently commendable. But here's a thought-provoking story to challenge that take.

I once encountered a couple who shared their experience with their daughter's recycling efforts. At first, they resisted her requests to recycle, but she persisted until they eventually joined in. The couple proudly referred to their daughter as a leader. However, when I (later) mentioned that leadership is defined by the presence of followers, they became visibly upset.

Surprised by their reaction, I pondered why they found it disturbing that their daughter wasn't considered a leader until they followed her. You see, being a leader isn't inherently good or bad. It's about having followers, regardless of the direction or impact. It can lead to positive change or, in some cases, even something harmful.

This discomforting realization forces us to reevaluate the extra meaning we attach to the word "leadership." When we imbue it with virtue, it confuses matters and blurs the distinction. To simplify things, let's strip away the misconceptions. Leadership is solely defined by the presence of followers.

So, the next time you ponder leadership, remember it's not about being good or bad. It's about your influence and the followers you gather along the way.

Yes, be a leader—a leader towards goodness. Get at it!

30

WHEN IN DOUBT,
SPREAD ACCOUNTABILITY OUT.

When in doubt, spread accountability out. But where should decisions truly belong? They should rest in the hands of those who face the consequences—the good, the bad, and the ugly.

Yet, what if we're uncertain about who should decide? That's when this guiding principle kicks in. When in doubt, spread accountability to those most impacted by the decision.

This doesn't mean sharing accountability for one thing among multiple people. We know that doesn't work! It's about recognizing complex situations with interlocking decisions that affect different individuals.

Entrepreneurs can also learn from this principle. Initially, founders do everything themselves. Maybe you can relate? However, as the organization grows, more people join the team, each accountable for different aspects of the business. I sometimes feel the impulse to show I'm not above any task, so I jump in to "help." But I missed considering my colleagues' desire to take ownership. When the founder trusts their team to handle tasks without jumping in to help, it empowers them and fosters a sense of pride in their work.

Spread accountability where it truly belongs, allowing individuals to take ownership and make decisions that drive success. By embracing this approach, we cultivate a culture of accountability and enable effective collaboration throughout the organization.

I often meet leaders who feel an obligation to have all the answers, even when they don't. They wear the responsibility of being the answer-guy or gal like a big burden on their backs. But how can any single person have all the answers? You may have lots of experience, smarts, and talent, which gives you many answers, but so what? You want to focus on what matters.

What's more important—being right or getting it right? Really think carefully about this. No, the answer isn't "both."

Do you really do such a terrible job of hiring that no one but you can make good decisions? I bet you have lots of insight sitting untapped across your team. The best way to access that genius is to use grassroots approaches to getting things built, decided on, and done.

This doesn't mean you aren't still involved in setting the guardrails around the solutions, but a grassroots approach shares the accountability for solving hard problems. By handing the baton to your colleagues, they have pride and ownership in the solutions. It only seems like a slower route to resolution.

I recall a company president saying to me, "But I can already see the solution; isn't it just quicker to tell them what needs to be done?"

No, actually. Aren't you motivated to implement things you play a part in creating? That's true for everyone. Yes, even you.

When in doubt, spread accountability out.

PEOPLE ENERGY PRINCIPLES
36 REFRAMES TO SHIFT HOW YOU THINK ABOUT PEOPLE & BUSINESS
SAME PEOPLE IN SAME ROLES = SAME PROBLEMS.

31 SAME PEOPLE
IN SAME ROLES = SAME PROBLEMS.

In business, having the right people in the right roles is key. You've heard it all before: Aces in their places, the right people in the right seats, and so on. It's common sense, really. Different folks excel at different things, so matching talents to tasks just makes sense.

But here's a kicker. When you've got the wrong people in the wrong roles, things don't fix themselves. Sure, you can give feedback and try to coach them up, but sometimes, that's just a Band-Aid on a bullet wound. You might tweak the role and change some responsibilities, but if the fit isn't right, you're just rearranging deck chairs on the Titanic.

This principle hit home for one of my coaching clients. He'd been dealing with performance issues from a team member for years. Finally, I dropped this truth bomb on him: "Same people in same roles = same problems." Silence. Then, a lightbulb moment. "Oh," he said, "I'm going to write that down."

Next time you face a performance issue, remember it might not be the person; it might just be the role. And if you don't make any changes to people or roles, don't expect your problems to improve. It just doesn't work that way.

PEOPLE ENERGY PRINCIPLES
36 REFRAMES TO SHIFT HOW YOU THINK ABOUT PEOPLE & BUSINESS
WHAT WE DO IS WHAT WE BELIEVE. ACT ON PURPOSE.

32 WHAT WE DO IS WHAT WE BELIEVE.
ACT ON PURPOSE.

What we do is what we believe. Actions speak louder than words, as they say. You can talk the talk, but if you ain't walking the walk, what's it all worth? And so on.

Our behaviors truly reflect our beliefs.

Words alone aren't enough to let people know what we stand for. Furthermore, our actions aren't just random occurrences; they manifest our deepest convictions.

You've heard it before: Talk is cheap. When someone's words don't sync up with their actions, it's the actions that carry the real weight.

If we're rigorously honest with ourselves, we all see through the smoke and mirrors straight to the truth of what's really going on. Don't you? Your team does.

Let's talk mission. It's the North Star guiding our ship through the stormy seas. But staying true to our mission isn't just about pretty words plastered on a slide deck. It's about living and breathing that mission daily with our actions.

Here's the deal: Stay on purpose. Walk the talk. Let your actions scream your beliefs from the mountaintops. That's how we roll, and that's how we keep our eyes locked on the prize.

Actions are what we believe. Stay on purpose.

PEOPLE ENERGY PRINCIPLES
36 REFRAMES TO SHIFT HOW YOU THINK ABOUT PEOPLE & BUSINESS
BUILD SYSTEMIC LIBERTY.

33 BUILD SYSTEMIC LIBERTY.

Picture this: The principle of building systemic liberty. We're talking about the sweet spot where structure elicits freedom—a game where every player can stretch their wings without clipping anyone else's.

We all crave the freedom to be ourselves and to pursue our passions without shackles. But it's easy to step on toes in a world where everyone's jostling for their slice of the pie, even when we don't mean to!

Now, imagine a game where the rules are designed to maximize freedom for all. It's like setting up guardrails tailored to each player's needs, ensuring they can navigate the course without crashing into each other.

This setup is not a zero-sum game where one person's gain is another's loss. No, it's a win-win scenario where everyone can thrive. It's a positive sum game.

Building systemic liberty isn't just about noble ideals; it's about creating an environment of freedom and opportunity. It's about fostering a culture where innovation, action, and truth-seeking are encouraged and expected. We know it's expected because we've designed for it!

Visualize an organization where freedom isn't a privilege but a presumption. Where every member is empowered to push boundaries and pursue excellence. Now, that's a goal worth striving for. It's hard to do but well worth it.

Build systemic liberty. Start today.

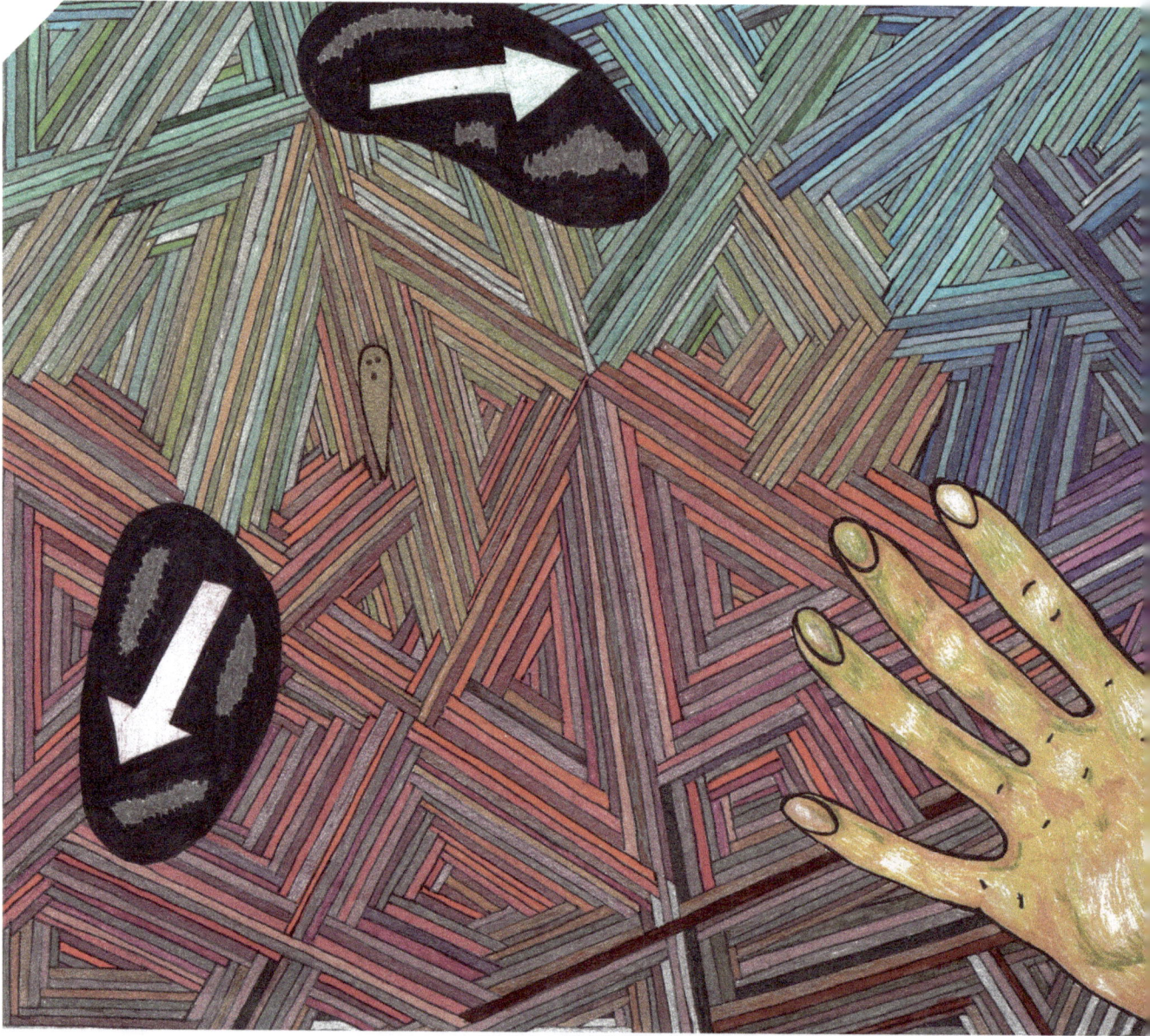

PEOPLE ENERGY PRINCIPLES
36 REFRAMES TO SHIFT HOW YOU THINK ABOUT PEOPLE & BUSINESS
WATCH OUT FOR THE DECIDER PROBLEM.

34 WATCH OUT FOR THE DECIDER PROBLEM.

Beware the Decider Problem, a sneaky little principle that creeps into decision-making processes unnoticed. What's a Decider Problem?

Picture this. You're nodding along to a policy not because it's a gem but because the big cheese in charge backs it. Does that make it a good policy? Maybe. How can you tell?

It's tricky to figure it out, but you are better equipped if you watch out for the decider problem.

When your stance on a policy hinges solely on your alignment with the decision-maker, you're skating on thin ice. It's like backing a horse because of the jockey, not the speed and stamina of the beast itself.

Instead, we dig into the fundamentals of the policy or solution. We peel back the layers and start asking the tough questions: Is this policy solid on its own merits? Or are we just riding the coattails of the decision-maker? Can we create a sound policy that doesn't rely on the particular beliefs or talents of the decider?

Mindlessly following authority leads us down a treacherous path. We must flex our critical thinking muscles, dissecting policies like a seasoned surgeon. It's not about who's calling the shots but whether those shots hit the mark, regardless of who's pulling the trigger. Designing decision processes that work no matter who's deciding is what we're looking for.

So, here's the takeaway: A policy worth its salt stands tall even when the decision-maker changes. We're talking about robust solutions that don't crumble at the first sign of a new face in the decider seat.

It's time to embrace only policies that stand strong on their own two feet. That, my friends, is how we build a future built to last.

Stay alert. Watch out for the Decider Problem!

PEOPLE ENERGY PRINCIPLES
36 REFRAMES TO SHIFT HOW YOU THINK ABOUT PEOPLE & BUSINESS
GRATITUDE IS CONTAGIOUS. PASS IT ON.

35 GRATITUDE IS CONTAGIOUS. PASS IT ON.

There's no way to overdose on sincere gratitude. Go ahead. Try it. What happens? How do you feel?

There is no downside to saying out loud what you are grateful for. When someone else does something you find helpful, useful, or otherwise positive, just mention it. You won't even have to tell others to show gratitude because when you do it, others will too.

It feels good to be grateful. It feels good to be appreciated.

The only way to do it wrong is to be insincere, which people will pick up on. Then, instead of feeling good and motivated, they feel manipulated and wary. Wary team members aren't as likely to perform as motivated team members. Heck, wary people generally won't trust you if you're insincere.

Gratitude is a power move.

Do you worry about coming off like a pushover? Too soft? Or maybe we fear that showing gratitude before things are perfect means supporting mediocrity. Nobody can be perfect. We can only take small, consistent steps towards getting better. You don't win by letting perfection get in the way of positive progress.

Is there a downside to gratitude?

What if we stop worrying about bad things for a minute and more bad things will happen? Or perhaps if we spend energy looking for good things, we'll miss fixing important bad things. We don't want to run around like a Pollyanna! How can we improve if we aren't constantly looking for things that are wrong?

Stop it. That's crazy talk. Sincere gratitude works.

Getting better means knowing what we should stop doing AND what we should *keep* doing. A gratitude focus helps us see what to keep doing, so unleash the positive people energy around you. Catch people doing things well. Share the positive feedback.

Be grateful; it's contagious. Pass it on.

PEOPLE ENERGY PRINCIPLES
36 REFRAMES TO SHIFT HOW YOU THINK ABOUT PEOPLE & BUSINESS
WHAT'S OLD IS NEW AGAIN. AGAIN.

36 WHAT'S OLD IS NEW AGAIN. AGAIN.

Who likes implementing flavor-of-the-month programs? What? This time it's different? maybe it is and maybe it isn't. Some of us like change. It's exciting and new. It might be amazing, and—well—the same will just be *the same*.

We often think things are so different nowadays that we need new solutions. And maybe sometimes we do. But…

Things that have worked well over a long period of time are likely to continue working. These things work well in many situations and through many changes. Sometimes we call these "principles" or "heuristics." Nicholas Nassim Taleb refers to them as "lindy."[1]

Try this mind-bender: When you encounter an idea that's been in circulation for a really long time, so long that it just sounds dull and inflexible, try to identify the original idea—the powerful principle beneath the words that have lost their oomph from over-repetition. Rather than look for a reason for it to be wrong—find what's right about it. And say that.

Need an example? It's become fashionable to hate hierarchies. There's a current belief that organizations will work better if we do away with all hierarchies because hierarchies can be bad, and everyone will be happier and more productive if we do away with bad hierarchies. However, hierarchies are never truly gone because we humans have to know how to orient ourselves to others and make decisions so that people agree on a path forward. It's an old, very old instinct. And that old instinct works.

What else is as old as the hills and still works? Consider what motivates people to do things—recognition, status, money, and security. These things have always worked, and they still work. No matter how much we search for intrinsic motivation or some other new-fangled magical silver bullet that doesn't require any time, energy, or resources from the employer, these principles work and should be the foundation of your organization if you want it to work. They are called fundamentals for a reason.

What's old is new again. Again.

[1] Nassim Nicholas Taleb. *Skin in the Game*. Random House, 2020.

APPENDIX.
THE TRUST ALGORITHM.

Trust is the foundation. Trust is the glue. Trust is the magic pixie fairy dust that makes your business better. We all love trust—all the kinds of trust—trust that people will do what they commit to do, trust that people will keep promises, trust that people will behave consistently, and trust that people will seek to benefit the greater good with their decisions. When you have it, trust feels good.

Lacking trust costs money.

Imagine running your business when you can't trust that people will do what they commit to, keep promises, behave consistently, and seek to benefit the greater good with their decisions. Ouch. When an organization recognizes that it has low trust, it can expect huge economic consequences. Everything will take longer, and everything will cost more because of the steps the organization will need to take to compensate for the lack of trust.

So, trust. Yay, trust!
How do we increase it?

Well, that's where things get a little unclear.

Is it heroic efforts on the part of the business' leaders to demonstrate the EQ, humility, and empathy that match today's ideal model of the best-ever-leader-not-manager? It sounds good and warm and fuzzy to have EQ, humility, and empathy. Yet normal humans, when they gain power, tend to experience a reduction in the need to demonstrate these very traits. So it seems true, but something is amiss.

Maybe it boils down to having the right character and personality traits. It's common to think that the cause of trust problems is one of character and personality. If we look around at the best and most effective leaders, wouldn't all of our most effective leaders be the very best at one particular set of traits if that is truly the differentiator? I don't know about you, but I don't see one style and one set of personality traits as being the best. I also see less effective managers display some otherwise honorable traits. This should add up if it's a real effect, but it doesn't.

High EQ, empathy, character, and a pleasant personality are desirable things to have in our leaders. Between one effective leader and another, we'd surely prefer to work with someone who has all of these things. But being pleasing to work with doesn't necessarily mean being more effective. Don't go thinking that this means that being purposely unpleasant to work with is the answer because that misses the point.

The point is to design your organization in a way that maximizes trust with a wide array of leadership styles and personality types.

Designing for trust.

I don't love solutions that call on heroics and overcoming our natural drives. I don't love solutions that moralize success and failure by implying that the existence of problems is necessarily the cause of somebody else's moral failings. For example, when a bank's practices place risk on future taxpayers, we jump to an answer that people in banking are just plain greedy and horrible. This finger-pointing might feel good (I do it too!), but it distracts us from the real causes of the problem.

Sure, there are likely greedy people in banking. There are greedy people everywhere. But greedy people aren't so much the cause as are the existence of financial institutions that became "too big to fail" and trading practices that disconnected risk and reward. Well, "That's banking," you might retort. I'm not in the banking business, or if I am, it's a small bank, and we're ethical. We aren't too big to fail. But guess what?

The same unfortunate dynamic is at work in your business.

When I see this moralizing, I am suspicious that we're missing something big—something systemic.

Like a fish doesn't notice the water it's swimming in, this big creator of organizational trust could be hiding right here, all around you. I propose, with an easy-to-remember algorithm, what that systemic thing is, so you can see the water.

Here's the algorithm that, when put into practice, leads to higher trust.

This algorithm is neither gospel nor conclusion. This is an idea. A model that might be useful in its simplicity and surprising in its comprehensiveness. A model that, when applied with rigor, will have a bigger impact on organization-wide trust than anything else you can do. There are other things you can do that also make a difference, but this one makes the BIGGEST DIFFERENCE.

Here it is: The organizational trust algorithm.

The more that accountability, authority, and capability are synced up for each and every role in an organization, the greater the trust. Here's a graphic to help you pick up what I'm putting down.

ACCOUNTABILITY = **AUTHORITY** = **CAPABILITY**

What does this even mean? It might even sound a little harsh and bureaucratic. A lot of people associate the word trust with softer ideas and calls to be more empathetic and humane, with calls to hug and sing "Kumbaya." And here I am, talking about mundane-sounding words like accountability, authority, and capability. But I tell you, accountability, authority, and capability are like the water the young fish couldn't see in David Foster Wallace's fish parable.[1]

Let me break it down for you.

An algorithm is a set of rules that precisely defines a sequence of operations. Hence, a trust algorithm is a set of rules that enhance trust. I should point out that an algorithm is usually applied in a computerized or otherwise automated fashion.

Here's where I break with tradition because a computer can't suss out these calculations. You are going to have to use your and your leaders' human brains and human judgments to determine if the accountability equals the authority of each role. You are going to have to use your and your leaders' human brains and human judgments to determine if the capability of the person in the role matches the authority and accountability designated to that role.

But don't sweat it. I'm going to help clear the fog for you.

First, let's define our terms.

Accountability — A person has accountability when they can be called to account for or be held responsible for their actions by another individual or body authorized to do so. Accountability also comes with recognition for the successful completion of those actions for which they are accountable, although it's the other side of the formula that we think about most.

Authority — A person has authority when they have legitimated power, that is to say, power vested in a person by virtue of their role to expend resources. These resources may be material, technical, or human. Informal power to expend resources that is not legitimated is not authority—it's manipulation.

---

[1] David Foster Wallace. "'This Is Water.'" *James Clear,* November 4, 2021. https://jamesclear.com/great-speeches/this-is-water-by-david-foster-wallace.

Capability — A person has capability when they have the ability to do the required work of a specific role at a given level at the present time. It is a function of the individual's skilled knowledge in the work area, the complexity of work processing, how much they value the work of the role, and the physical ability to carry out the required behaviors.

(Definitions informed by Elliott Jaques' definitions of these terms from the glossary of his book titled "The Life and Behavior of Living Organisms.")[2]

The more these three things are equal and in sync, the better your business' foundation of trust will be. Make sense? We should be simpatico so far. I don't think I've said anything controversial here.

All the ways it goes right and wrong.

Now let's talk about how it works when each pair of variables is in sync, and the symptoms of when they are misalignment. See if you recognize some of these conditions in your business.

ACCOUNTABILITY   **AUTHORITY**

When Accountability and Authority are in sync.

When <u>accountability and authority</u> are aligned, the person in the role can do the things that enable them to succeed or fail. They can't point to system-level problems and say, "I could have succeeded if only…" This is so obvious it's tempting to believe that it's commonly in place. Hold that thought while we describe the symptoms you see when accountability and authority get out of sync.

When Accountability and Authority are out of sync.

When <u>accountability > authority</u>, we experience stress and frustration because we're being held to account for outcomes over which we have little control. Not enough control. Success or failure feels more like a function of luck and accident. To gain some control over our destiny, we may find it necessary to rely on coercion and influence along informal lines to get things done. It creates a web of deceit and confusion. It creates poisonous "politics" — the kind of politics that your well-meaning colleagues joined your smaller business to avoid. And that's a tragedy.

[2] Jaques, Elliott. *The Life and Behavior of Living Organisms.* Bloomsbury Publishing USA, 2001.

When <u>authority > accountability</u>, we have a different set of symptoms. The problems mainly arise when things aren't going well because it's the lack of consequences that encourage actions that are dysfunctional, serve the wrong end, and are risky-to-the-business. This divorcing of benefit and risk is called a *moral hazard*[3] in economic circles, and, far from being an irrelevant abstraction, this concept applies when your people and operations practices cause authority to outpace accountability. For example, a team member has the authority to make decisions about the use of resources that cause obstacles for success to another part of the business. We've seen these power dynamics happen in banks (like the Wells Fargo fiasco). Any time you hear rumblings that so-and-so doesn't have to play by the same rules as other people, you might have the same dynamic in your business. Don't let it go unaddressed.

ACCOUNTABILITY   **CAPABILITY**

When Accountability and Capability are in sync.

When the accountability of the role is matched by the capability of the person, you have a role/person fit. The role is the right size, the person has the necessary skilled knowledge, and the person is willing to do the work. You have the right person in the right seat. Good results are likely to follow.

When Accountability and Capability are out of sync.

When <u>accountability > capability</u>, it's a bad situation. In the absence of dumb luck, the person is doomed to fail. The person is in over their head because they lack the ability, willingness, or interest in the requirements of the role. When you have these symptoms due to over-promotion, you have what is called the *Peter Principle*.[4] If the person in over their head is a manager, they will be unable to give proper context to team members, and the team loses connection to larger goals and strategies. Problem signs are a kind of tunnel vision on the part of the leader and an inability to adjust in the face of normal change. They will swear

[3] Contributors to Wikimedia projects. "Moral Hazard - Wikipedia." *Wikipedia*, April 25, 2024. https://en.wikipedia.org/wiki/Moral_hazard.

[4] Contributors to Wikimedia projects. "Peter Principle - Wikipedia." *Wikipedia*, April 2, 2024. https://en.wikipedia.org/wiki/Peter_principle.

that changes were impossible to anticipate and finger-point at their peers and outside influences as the cause of their leadership errors. These behavioral frustrations quickly turn into top and bottom-line business problems. Not good!

When capability > accountability, you have an entirely different set of problems. At first glance, you might even think that having excess capability would be a good thing. Guaranteed success! But no. It won't be long before boredom sets in, and the over-capable colleague expands the role without permission and perhaps without awareness that they are doing so. Resources will be applied where you don't intend them. They won't "roll up their sleeves" and do the doing—inclined, instead, to do the planning and delegating. These things are frustrating for the manager of the over-capable person. As a result, the manager often succumbs to the temptation to paint the over-capable colleague as insubordinate, NOT a team player, and a "poor culture fit." It's an uncomfortable situation that breaks down trust and relationships, typically ending with a high-capability person leaving your business with a bad taste in their mouth. They probably won't say nice things on Glassdoor.

AUTHORITY   CAPABILITY

When Authority and Capability are in sync.

People can do what they are authorized to do. People are willing to do what they are authorized to do. The person's talent, skills, and interests are matched up with the nature of the work. They are going to feel good about the work they do. They will feel adequately challenged. The need to use informal methods of influence will be minimal.

When Authority and Capability are out of sync.

When authority > capability, you end up with either a little dictator or general ineptitude. Which option you get depends on the leadership style of the person. In either case, you don't get the results you are paying for. If you are the manager, you might find yourself doing the employee's work for them and getting pulled into the weeds a lot more than you want. If you report to someone who has more authority than capability, you'll feel adrift because they don't make decisions, or you'll feel micro-managed to the ends of your patience. In either case, making this mistake is a great way to get rid of highly capable people because capable people have alternatives to working with incompetent people.

When capability > authority, everything looks like it's coming up roses — at first. Then, by about six months in, you see signs of the person working *around* the structure rather than with it, manipulating situations so that they are more interesting for them. This scenario leads people to take the skill of influencing without authority well past the healthy point. If they are blocked from doing this, they'll complain about boredom and the decisions made by their peers and bosses.

The relevance of the trust algorithm to your business.

At least some of the symptoms of accountability, authority, and capability getting out of sync should sound familiar. I've never come across a business that doesn't have pockets of these symptoms. In my role, people tell me stories about how things go wrong where they work. They tell me their frustrations and criticisms, even when they mostly love their colleagues and jobs. Every criticism and complaint I hear has, at its roots, a failing of the trust algorithm. Every. Single. One. We need to do something!

Can these problems ever be solved?

It's hard to solve these — for sure. It takes constant vigilance with the trust algorithm at the forefront of our minds. What if — we fear — it's just too hard? What if these problems can't be solved, so why try? Maybe it's better to just be pragmatic and do things the traditional way.

That's fine if you don't have high expectations for your business.

There are reasons that we regularly fail to notice when the trust algorithm gets a little off-kilter. These reasons include mental traps that hide the truth from our view if we aren't careful.

So that you don't get caught in the snake pit, let's cover some of the big ones.

Common traps that distract you from the problem.

TRAP #1: Trust because of positional authority.

When confronted with a lack of trust, some leaders take it personally and blame the employee. They worry, "What if people don't trust me as a leader?! That would be awful! They should trust me BECAUSE I'm the leader, right?" If capability is synced with authority for all leaders' roles, that mindset will be mostly fine. But you wouldn't want your judgments to NEVER be questioned, would you? Ever? If you see this dynamic occur in your business, it's a sign to use the trust algorithm to see if you're missing something.

TRAP #2: The role of personality in conflict.

When people describe workplace conflicts and breakdowns in trust, they are often couched as "personality conflicts." That's because the tenor and tone of the conflicts take the shape of the personalities involved. It's highly visible; personality is hard to ignore. Yet, if you run the conflict situation through the trust algorithm, you'll almost always find that the cause of the conflict is a breakdown between accountability, authority, or capability. But what about personality, doesn't that matter? Less than you think.

TRAP #3: We just need to learn conflict resolution skills.

Chalk this one up as another Band-Aid to fix a broken arm. This isn't to say that people shouldn't have conflict resolution skills; they should. Having them is part of the capability requirements for any leadership role. Most any role, actually. Sometimes, a conflict *is* nothing more than a skills issue, and to solve it, people involved simply need to learn conflict resolution skills.

Guess what the best conflict resolution skill is? It's using the trust algorithm. Yep. Solving an endemic trust problem with conflict skills training is like doing laps so you can swim upstream and go backward slower. When authority, accountability, and capability are synced, it's like swimming with the flow. And that's better.

TRAP #4: Confusing authority and accountability.

We already defined the terms, so I won't do that again here. The trap is that, in our common parlance, we use the words authority and accountability interchangeably. We aren't precise with our language, which is unsurprising, given its difficulty, but this particular brand of confusion fogs up our organizational glasses. For example, putting words on a job description and an organizational chart might grant accountability, but it doesn't ensure authority. Get clear on the difference between these two concepts.

TRAP #5: Misunderstanding what capability means.

The biggest mistake is believing that training can solve any capability mismatch. Training helps build skilled knowledge, presuming the person values the work and cognitive power. When I use the word capability here, I mean more than just skilled knowledge. In the definition I provided earlier, there are many components to capability. Some capability gaps can be rectified with training and experience, while others cannot. Sometimes, a poor capability fit can be solved by re-working the role to better match the person's special stack of talents, interests, and abilities. Sometimes not.

Let's wrap this up.

So, where does this leave us? We've discussed the components of the trust algorithm — authority, accountability, and capability. We've talked about what it looks like when the components are in sync. We've also discussed the symptoms that emerge when they aren't so you can recognize them in your own business. We've described the common mental traps that fool us into misdiagnosing what are trust algorithm misalignments.

How do you apply the trust algorithm in YOUR business?

This algorithm is a simple, comprehensive heuristic, but it requires that you *convert the concepts into concrete observations and actions*. I've attempted to give you enough guidance to reframe almost any people problem you see in your business but providing specific actions to apply in your business is beyond the scope of this book. I aim to help you bypass the trap of solving symptoms and seeing the same problem themes occur again and again.

When you think about people and trust problems through the lens of the model, you solve people problems by getting to the root of the issues. You can do it! Post the algorithm where you'll see it every day, so it's a part of how you think about your people and operations. When you need help, call me.

THANK YOU FOR READING MY BOOK!

Your journey to unleashing people energy starts here!

Scan the QR code below to access a special gift—What's available changes from time to time.
It might be an exclusive print (for the first 20 responders), early access to new insights,
or a Free People Energy audit to help amp your growth-readiness.

Don't miss out—Scan now and see what's waiting for you!

SCAN ME

www.ingramcontent.com/pod-product-compliance
Lightning Source LLC
Chambersburg PA
CBHW050344230326
41458CB00102B/6353

9 781967 424177